The Music Lover's Quotation Book

The Music Lover's Quotation Book

A Lyrical Companion

Compiled and edited by:
KATHLEEN KIMBALL
ROBIN PETERSEN
KATHLEEN JOHNSON

SOUND AND VISION
TORONTO

Preface

It may be true, as Camille Saint-Saëns said, that "there is nothing more difficult than talking about music"; nevertheless, like love, music has inspired many interesting comments. Perhaps just as difficult is keeping silent about something so wonderful. Granted, passions are seldom easily captured in words; but perhaps this is why what is said is fascinating to us. What has been expressed in a clever, insightful, amusing or beautiful way about this ephemeral medium?

As musicians and lovers of literature, it has been delightful for us as friends to meet, pool our quote collections and arrange them into subtopics of "conversation." Happily, with quotes it is possible to bring together personalities separated by centuries and continents. Thus, in our composers section an array of widely varying creators tell how they are inspired. In "music and love", poets, musicians and others give lush statements. When we could, we included opposing views—for instance, Robert Browning and P.J. Bailey disagreed on the truth obtainable in music, as did George Gershwin and Maxim Gorky on jazz.

But another charming advantage of quotes is that they can be read in any order. At any point one can find in these pages a pithy or witty gem by a "noted" person. To us, some quotes are like little poems, complete in themselves. Whether music is your profession, your escape, or an occasional pleasure in your life, we hope you enjoy this book.

Kathleen Kimball
Robin Peterson
Kathleen Johnson

Contents

origins...

Nothing exists without music, for the universe itself is said to have been framed by a kind of harmony of sounds, and the heaven itself revolves under the tones of that harmony.

ISODORE OF SEVILLE

Then the Lord answered Job out of the whirlwind, and said, "Where wast thou when I laid the foundations of the earth... when the morning stars sang together, and all the sons of God shouted for joy?"

JOB 38: 1,4,7

The discovery of song and the creation of musical instruments both owed their origin to a human impulse which lies much deeper than conscious intention: the need for rhythm in life... the need is a deep one, transcending thought, and disregarded at our peril.

RICHARD BAKER

Music moves us, and we know not why; we feel the tears but cannot trace the source. Is it the language of some other state, born of its memory? For what can wake the soul's strong instinct of another world like music?

L. E. LANDON

Music is... a labyrinth with no beginning and no end, full of new paths to discover, where mystery remains eternal.

PIERRE BOULEZ

1

Music produces a kind of pleasure which human nature cannot do without.

CONFUCIOUS

There is always music in the garden, if only we have ears to hear it.

UNKNOWN

Come, follow me into the realm of music. Here is the iron fence which separates the earthly from the eternal. Have you undone the fetters and thrown them away? Now come. It is not as it was before when we stepped into a strange country; we soon learnt to know everything there and nothing surprised us any longer. Here there is no end to the astonishments, and yet from the beginning we feel it is homelike...

FERRUCCIO BUSONI, *in a letter to his wife*

what music is...

The very existence of music is wonderful, I might even say miraculous. Its domain is between thought and phenomena. Like a twilight mediator, it hovers between spirit and matter, related to both, yet differing from each. It is spirit, but it is spirit subject to the measurement of time. It is matter, but it is matter that can dispense with space.

HEINRICH HEINE

Music, the mosaic of the air.

ANDREW MARVELL

Music is the medicine of the mind.

JOHN LOGAN

2

I could imagine a music whose rarest charm should consist in its complete divorce from the Good and Bad;—only that its surface might be ruffled, as it were, by a longing for home, by variable golden shadows and tender frailties:— an Art which should see fleeing toward it, from afar off, the hues of a perishing moral world become well nigh incomprehensible, and which should be hospitable and profound enough to harbor such belated fugitives.

FRIEDRICH NIETZSCHE

Music is the only innocent and unpunished passion.

SYDNEY SMITH

Everything is music for the born musician. Everything that throbs, or moves or stirs, or palpitates... everything that is, is music; all that is needed is that it should be heard.

ROMAIN ROLLAND

Song is the pen of the soul.

RABBI CHAIM DRIZIN, *at funeral for tenor Jan Peerce*

Music has been my playmate, my lover, and my crying towel.

BUFFY SAINTE-MARIE

Music is indivisable. The dualism of feeling and thinking must be resolved to a state of unity in which one thinks with the heart and feels with the brain.

GEORGE SZELL

3

Music washes away from the soul the dust of everyday life.
BERTHOLD AUERBACH

If this word 'music' is sacred and reserved for eighteenth and nineteenth century instruments, we can substitute a more meaningful term: organization of sound.
JOHN CAGE

Music is the wine which inspires one to new generative processes, and I am Bacchus who presses out this glorious wine for mankind and makes them spiritually drunken.
LUDWIG VAN BEETHOVEN

music and art...

All art constantly aspires towards the condition of music.
WALTER PATER

... music—so different than painting—is the art which we enjoy most in company with others. A symphony, presented in a room with one other listener, would please him but little.
ROBERT SCHUMANN

Art is the triumph over chaos.
JOHN CHEEVER

4

The aesthetic principle is the same in every art, only the material differs.
ROBERT SCHUMANN

... and to us rose Shelley with liquid music in the word.
ROBERT BRIDGES

Any great work of art... revives and readapts time and space, and the measure of its success is the extent to which it makes you an inhabitant of that world—the extent to which it invites you in and lets you breathe its strange, special air.
LEONARD BERNSTEIN, *What makes Opera Grand?*

Chaos is a friend of mine.
BOB DYLAN

... I'm convinced that in a healthy society, artistic norms should be constantly under question, which is not of course, to deny the need for continuity.
EARLE BROWN

The essence of all art is having pleasure giving pleasure.
MIKHAIL BARYSHNIKOV

Art is the perpetual motion of illusion. The highest purpose of art is to inspire. What else can you do? What else can you do for any one but inspire them?
BOB DYLAN

music and language...

When words leave off, music begins.
HEINRICH HEINE

Music is well said to be the speech of angels.
THOMAS CARLYLE

Music is the vapor of art. It is to poetry what reverie is to thought, what fluid is to solid, what the ocean of clouds is to the ocean of waves.
VICTOR HUGO

Music rots when it gets too far from the dance. Poetry atrophies when it gets too far from music.
EZRA POUND

... Music has a poetry all of its own, and that poetry is called melody.
JOSHUA LOGAN

Chamber music—a conversation between friends.
CATHERINE DRINKER BOWEN

The irrepressible spirit that made his playing seem like good conversation... is the Rubinstein legacy for pianists, if they can pick up their heads from the keyboard long enough to claim it.
DONAL HENAHAN

His [Niccoló Paganini's] bow perfectly talks. It remonstrates, supplicates, answers, holds a dialogue.

LEIGH HUNT

The language of tones belongs equally to all mankind, and melody is the absolute language in which the musician speaks to every heart.

RICHARD WAGNER

Music is the universal language of mankind.

HENRY WADSWORTH LONGFELLOW

Because I am a storyteller I live by words. Perhaps music is a purer art form. It may be that when we communicate with life on another planet, it will be through music, not through language or words.

MADELEINE L'ENGLE

Obviously, we cannot come too early to music. And those who come too late suffer the same fate as adults who struggle to learn a second language, and who are forever uncomfortable with its pronunciation, grammar, syntax, rhythm, and idiom.

DEENA and BERNARD ROSENBURG

There is nothing more difficult than talking about music.

CAMILLE SAINT-SAËNS

8

I must say Bernard Shaw is greatly improved by music.

T.S. ELIOT, *on being asked for his opinion of the opening night performance of My Fair Lady*

Aside from purely technical analysis, nothing can be said about music, except when it is bad; when it is good, one can only listen and be grateful.

W. H. AUDEN

For is not music a language? And of what is it the language? Is it not the language of the dream world, the world beyond thought?

ROBERTSON DAVIES, *The Lyre of Orpheus*

music and philosophy...

Without music, life would be a mistake. ...I would only believe in a God that knew how to dance.

FRIEDRICH NIETZSCHE

Rhythm and melody enter into the soul of the well-instructed youth and produce there a certain mental harmony hardly obtainable in any other way. ...thus music, too, is concerned with the principles of love in their application to harmony and rhythm.

PLATO

Music is essentially useless, as life is.

GEORGE SANTAYANA

10

I despise a world which does not feel that music is a higher revelation than all wisdom and philosophy.

LUDWIG VAN BEETHOVEN

I try to be an atheist, but it's very hard. God is what makes you aspire beyond yourself, aspire incredibly. God to me is what stops you from slicing the jugular because you choose not to. God is the Sistine Chapel, the *Ninth Symphony*, God is Bach and the Prado Museum! And this is what I've tried to show in my work.

JOSÉ LIMÓN

It [music] excites in my mind no ideas, and hinders me from contemplating my own.

SAMUEL JOHNSON

Beethoven has sometimes been called a philosophical musician, but if that means he was a philosopher it is certainly untrue. Music can no more express philosophical ideas than it can express scientific ideas. And nothing that Beethoven wanted to express can be called a philosophy. The states of consciousness he expresses, his reactions to perceptions and experiences are not ideas. Belief in a Heavenly Father cannot be expressed in music; what can be expressed and with unexampled power, is the state of soul that such a belief, sincerely held, may arouse.

J.W.N. SULLIVAN, *Beethoven: his Spiritual Development*

To some it is Napoleon, to some it is a philosophical struggle, to me it is an *allegro con brio*.

ARTURO TOSCANINI, *on Beethoven's Eroica*

11

Classical philosophy did not censor the singers. It persuaded them.

ALLAN BLOOM, *The Closing of the American Mind*

I don't think one can persuade anybody to listen to music, go to a museum, or read philosophy. It must come from within.

PINCHAS ZUKERMAN

Music, of all the arts, stands in a special region, unlit by any star but its own, and utterly without meaning... except its own.

LEONARD BERNSTEIN, *The Joy of Music*

I cannot recall an experience that has embodied so much of what I consider to be the true significance of the greater religion we all share.

REVEREND R. YANDELL, *on hearing the Mormon Tabernacle Choir*

I have a sweet tooth for song and music. This is my Polish sin.

POPE JOHN PAUL II, *listening to folk-rock hymns on a visit to Poland, 1979*

music and science...

Music is the soul of geometry.

PAUL CLAUDEL

12

Most people rather think of music as an art. But in reality music partakes of both art and science... every time a printed score is brought to life it has to be re-created through different sound machines called musical instruments.

EDGAR VARÈSE

Albert Einstein played the violin with some enthusiasm. He once played for Gregor Piatigorsky, the distinguished cellist, and he asked him: "How well did I play?" Pitigorsky replied: "You played *relatively* well."

ROBERT GIDDINGS, *Musical Quotes and Anecdotes*

Definitely not, but I wish it did. Why, I can hardly add two and two.

RALPH VAUGHAN WILLIAMS, *when asked if the phenomenon of mathematicians often being good musicians worked in the reverse*

For a number of years now my music has been influenced by the great power and the beauty of nature and man's responsibility to preserve and cherish it. *Music for Heaven and Earth* is the embodiment of my feelings of wonder, fear and awe of the vast mysterious black void of outer space, love and tenderness at the sight of our rising, beautiful, fragile earth from the desolate surface of the moon, and finally, a celebration of our unique place in the starry heavens.

ALEXINA LOUIE, *on her world premiere with the Toronto Symphony, 1991*

13

In art, and in the higher ranges of science, there is a feeling of harmony which underlies all endeavor. There is no true greatness in art or science without that sense of harmony.

ALBERT EINSTEIN, *on the connection between music and mathematics*

Musical sound lies within the very hearts of the atoms.

DR. DONALD H. ANDREWS, *Symphony of Life*

music and politics...

In my view, the composer, just as the poet, the sculptor or the painter, is in duty bound to serve Man, the people. He must beautify life and defend it. He must be a citizen first and foremost, so that his art might consciously extol human life and lead man to a radiant future.

SERGEI PROKOFIEV

The city is built
To music, therefore never built at all,
And therefore built forever.

ALFRED LORD TENNYSON

Certain keys, tonalities, and melodic formulas fortify the human character; others may weaken it. Musical training is a more potent instrument than any other, because rhythm and harmony find their way into the secret places of the soul.

PLATO, *The Republic*

14

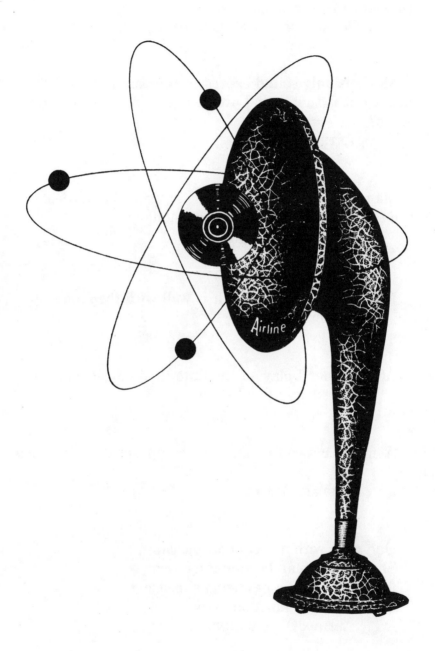

I have found among my papers a sheet... in which I call architecture frozen music.
JOHANN WOLFGANG GOETHE

Music is only sound expressing certain patterns, so to what extent is that sound architecture and to what extent theatre?
ARTHUR BROWN

Man will begin to recover the moment he takes art as seriously as physics, chemistry or money.
ERNST LEVY

If the King loves music, it is well with the land.
MENCIUS

After dinner I play on the flute to aid digestion...
FREDERICK II OF PRUSSIA

A nation creates music—the composer only arranges it.
MIKHAIL GLINKA

One man with a dream, at pleasure,
Shall go forth and conquer a crown;
And three with a new song's measure
Can trample a kingdom down.
ARTHUR O' SHAUGHNESSY, Ode

16

Noisy politicians confuse the world. I sing to the moon alone.

Yü Hsuen-Chi

The popular song is America's greatest ambassador.

Sammy Cahn

The history of a people is found in its songs.

George Jellenik

... Songs are sneaky things. They can slip across borders. Proliferate in prisons. Penetrate hard shells... I always believed that the right song at the right moment could change history.

Pete Seeger

We must, once and for all reject the worthless interference in musical compositions as it is practiced by musical establishments. Problems of composition cannot be solved by official bureaucratic methods... Let the individual artist be trusted more fully and not constantly supervised and suspected.

Aram Khachaturian, *after Stalin's death*

To sit on a log or stools or tables in the crude old attap-roofed kitchen, with only one light, and then to be lifted right out that atmosphere with this music is sheer joy. It is easy to forget one is a prisoner.

Betty Jeffrey, *Women Beyond the Wire*

17

Tell a man what he may sing and he is still half free; even all free, if he never wanted to sing it. But tell him what he must sing, take up his time with it so that his true voice cannot sound even in secret—there, I have seen is slavery.

MARY RENAULT

As blended voices filled the air
The soul could soar to worlds more fair,
Escape from prison bonds.

MARGARET DRYBURGH, *creator of women's vocal orchestra during internment in WWII Japanese prison camp*

Music, of all the liberal arts, has the greatest influence over the passions, and it is that to which the legislator ought to give the greatest encouragement.

NAPOLEON BONAPARTE

Through him, [Chopin], Poland has obtained a seat and vote in the great musical parliment of the nations. Annihilated politically, it will ever continue to flower in our art.

ROBERT SCHUMANN

I must study politics and war that my sons may have liberty to study mathematics and philosophy... in order to give their children a right to study painting, poetry and music.

JOHN ADAMS

18

Piano playing is more difficult than statesmanship. It is harder to wake emotions in ivory keys than it is in human beings.

IGNACY PADEREWSKI

Where the people sing, no man is ever robbed.

J.G. SEUME

Last year more Americans went to symphonies [symphony concerts] than went to baseball games. This may be viewed as an alarming statistic, but I think that both baseball and the country will endure.

JOHN F. KENNEDY

All the disorders, all the wars we behold throughout the world occur only because of the neglect to learn music. Does not war result from lack of unison among men? Thus, were all men to learn music, would not this be the means of agreement between them and of seeing universal peace reign all over the world?

MOLIÈRE

Western music is like the sun. All over the world, the sunset is different, but the beauty is the same. Maybe there is a way to make a marriage between this Oriental blood and Western music... It's so strong and logical that it is easy for every nationality to learn.

SEIJI OZAWA

We feel this urgency. All of us, all over the world, adults, children, writers, musicians—have to talk about peace because we so desperately need it.

TUCK ANDRESS and PATTI CATHCART

A song has a few rights the same as ordinary citizens... if it happens to feel like flying where humans cannot fly... to scale mountains that are not there, who shall stop it?

CHARLES IVES

music and food...

To some people music is like food; to others like medicine; to others like a fan.

Tales of the Arabian Nights

If music be the food of love, play on...

SHAKESPEARE, *Twelfth Night*

Eating, loving, singing and digesting are, in truth, the four acts of the comic opera known as life, and they pass like bubbles of a bottle of champagne. Whoever lets them break without having enjoyed them is a complete fool.

GIOACHINO ROSSINI

There's sure no passion in the human soul, but finds its food in music.

GEORGE LILLO

21

Music, moody food
of us that trade in love.
SHAKESPEARE, *Antony and Cleopatra*

A concert should be made up like a menu...you wouldn't give a guest veal, beef, and chicken in one meal, nor should you give three sonatas in a concert. There must be fish, meat, salad and dessert.
ARTUR RUBINSTEIN

It's nice to eat a good hunk of beef but you want a light dessert, too.
ARTHUR FIEDLER

I always have a boiled egg. A three-minute egg. Do you know how I time it? I bring it to the boil and then conduct the overture to the *Marriage of Figaro*. Three minutes exactly.
SIR JOHN BARBIROLLI

Clean living keeps me in shape. Righteous thoughts are my secret. And New Orleans home cooking.
FATS DOMINO

music and love...

I am not handsome, but when women hear me play, they come crawling to my feet.
NICCOLÓ PAGANINI

22

I have applied
Sweet mirth, and music, and have tried
A thousand other arts beside,
To drive thee from my darkened breast,
Thou, who has banished all my rest.
　　　ANNE FINCH

Music and woman I cannot but give way to, whatever
my business is.
　　　SAMUEL PEPYS

Which of the two powers, love or music, is able to lift
man to the sublimest heights? It is a great question, but it
seems to me that one might answer it thus: love cannot
express the idea of music, while music may give an idea of
love. Why separate the one from the other? They are the
two wings of the soul.
　　　HECTOR BERLIOZ

Are we not formed, as notes of music are,
For one another, though dissimilar?
　　　PERCY BYSSHE SHELLEY

... What I feel
Here in this room, desiring you, thinking of your blue-
shadowed silk
　Is music.
　　　WALLACE STEVENS, *Peter Quince at the Clavier*

24

He is gone, who knew the music of my soul.
HSUEH T'AO

If you had asked me whether I had ever found complete happiness in love, I should have replied no, and again, no. Besides, I think the answer to this question is to be heard in my music. If, however, you ask me whether I have felt the whole power and inexpressible stress of love, I must reply, yes, yes, yes; for often I have striven to render in music all the anguish and the bliss of love.
PYOTR ILYICH TCHAIKOVSKY, *in a letter to Nadezhda von Meck*

Oh, Marcia... your long blonde beauty... God lives like music in the skin...
RICHARD BRAUTIGAN, *Gee, You're So Beautiful That it's Starting to Rain*

The entire works of Chopin present a motley surface of ranting hyperbole and excruciating cacophony... There is an excuse at present for Chopin's delinquencies: he is entrammelled in the enthralling bonds of that arch-enchantress, George Sand, celebrated equally for the number and excellence of her romances and her lovers.
Review in Musical World

It was like the first time I ever made love. Terrifying to contemplate, wonderful when it happened and all too brief. And something I'll never forget.
GAMBLE ROGERS, *on his debut at Carnegie Hall*

25

... Our meeting is similar
to the way I feel about Bach.
His music is so intricate yet so simple
I can't help but try to understand it.
So vital I can't be without it.
And so emotional I want to sit down and cry....
W. FREDERICK YOHE, *Someone Is
About to Happen to You*

When I play, I make love—it is the same thing.
ARTUR RUBINSTEIN

What passion cannot music raise and quell!
JOHN DRYDEN

The music broke from the piano like clear cold water
from a prophet-touched rock, pouring and splashing
around us while her fingers leaped and spread, curled and
stiffened and melted and flickered in magic pass and
streaked lightning above the keyboard. Never before had
she played for me... because we were lovers now, was she
free to play...?
RICHARD BACH, *The Bridge Across Forever*

On stage, I make love to 25,000 different people, then I
go home alone.
JANIS JOPLIN

Music is love in search of a word.
SIDNEY LANIER

music and money...

It is a mistakenly romantic notion to read into music personal statements of tragic experience which may be synchronous in the composer's life with the creation of the music in question. Mozart composed music of radiant vivacity, sparkle and wit at times when he was crippled by neglect, debt, and the awful discouragement of living his whole life insufficiently compensated and recognized.
MARCIA DAVENPORT, *Mozart*

Is there a basic split between the cosmic world of imagination and the hostile world of commercial practicality?
KEVIN KINCAID

The amount of money one needs is terrifying...
LUDWIG VAN BEETHOVEN

Only become a musician if there is absolutely no other way you can make a living.
KIRKE MECHAM, *on his life as a composer*

A wise friend of my father's had said to me: "You should not go into music unless it is a compulsion. In the end all you really have as a center is the music itself. Make sure that you have to be with it every day. If that's true then you should become a musician."
MICHAEL TILSON THOMAS

27

I did not choose my profession, it chose me. Since childhood it has grown between me and people. My music is all one love letter, but to whom?

NED ROREM

When I was young I wanted to play the guitar. But I was told it wasn't respectable. My father broke three guitars to stop me from practicing... I received from heaven a gift for music and could not do anything but music. The vocation was compulsory.

ANDRÉS SEGOVIA

I've never known a musician who regretted being one. Whatever deceptions life may have in store for you, music itself is not going to let you down.

VIRGIL THOMSON, *commencement address at the New England Conservatory of Music*

Art was not created as a way to riches. Strive to become a true artist; all else will take care of itself.

ROBERT SCHUMANN

I would rather play *Chiquita Banana* and have my swimming pool than play Bach and starve.

XAVIER CUGAT

I've got a car, a motorcycle, a truck, a house—what more could I possibly want?

BRUCE SPRINGSTEEN

28

Of course, we want to make more money and know where it goes. Why be naive about it? Why die like Stephen Foster, in the Bowery, slitting his wrists after writing all those wonderful standards?
GLENN FREY

Of course I'm ambitious. What's wrong with that? Otherwise you sleep all day.
RINGO STARR

An artist, in giving a concert, should not demand an entrance fee but should ask the public to pay, just before leaving as much as they like. From the sum he would be able to judge what the world thinks of him—and we would have fewer mediocre concerts.
KIT COLEMAN, *Kit Coleman: Queen of Hearts*

[Musicians] talk of nothing but money and jobs. Give me businessmen every time. They really are interested in music and art.
JEAN SIBELIUS, *explaining why he rarely invited musicians to his home*

The opera always loses money. That's as it should be. Opera has no business making money.
SIR RUDOLPH BING, *New York Times*

What's money? A man is a success if he gets up in the morning and gets to bed at night and in between he does what he wants to.
BOB DYLAN

30

For the first time in history, the artist is realizing financial success in his lifetime.

JOE WALSH

The apartment of Georges Enesco in Paris was less than modest. It was poverty itself. Yet, it contained certain riches and an extraordinary musician... As I prepared to leave, Enesco turned to his piano and announced that he would treat me to something light and gay. Then with the knuckles of his crippled hands, he played a charming little Chinese tune. It still haunts my memory whenever I think of that indomitable old man who lived, almost literally I think, on the nourishment of music.

JOUSEF KARSH, *Portraits of Greatness*

music's effects...

Nothing on earth is so well suited to make the sad merry, the merry sad, to give courage to the despairing, to make the proud humble, to lessen envy and hate, as music.

MARTIN LUTHER

When people hear good music, it makes them homesick for something they never had and never will have.

EDGAR W. HOWE

Most people use music as a couch; they want to be pillowed on it, relaxed and consoled for the stress of daily living. But serious music was never meant to be soporific.

AARON COPLAND

31

[Johnson] owned to me that he was very insensible to the power of musick. I told him that it affected me to such a degree, as often to agitate my nerves painfully, producing in my mind alternate sensations of pathetic dejection, so that I was ready to shed tears; and of daring resolution, so that I was inclined to rush into the thickest part of the battle.

JAMES BOSWELL

Sir, [to Boswell] I would never hear it if it made me such a fool.

SAMUEL JOHNSON

We love music for the buried hopes, the garnered memories, the tender feelings it can summon at a touch.

L.E. LANDON

When I hear music, I flutter, and am the scene of life, as a fleet of merchantmen when the wind rises.

HENRY DAVID THOREAU, *Journal*

If the piece works poetically, it takes me down a new path from beginning to end. Each piece should be like a journey—and every journey is different.

EARLE BROWN

Music should strike fire from the heart of man and bring tears to the eyes of woman.

LUDWIG VAN BEETHOVEN

32

Feelings accompany our apprehension of a piece of music in the way they accompany the events of our life.
LUDWIG WITTGENSTEIN

Music hath charms to soothe the savage beast.
JAMES BRAMSTON

Ten years, ten years, I've been waiting for that A on the cellos!
ALEXIS EMMANUEL CHABRIER, *bursting into tears at the thrill of hearing the prelude to Wagner's Tristan and Isolde*

I had the sensation of letting myself be penetrated and invaded—a really sensual delight that resembles rising on the air or tossing upon the sea...
CHARLES BAUDELAIRE, *on hearing Wagner*

Music has brought me some of the highest moments of my life. I don't even hear the music. I don't hear the notes. I'm not aware that someone has turned on a tape machine or that a record is playing—I'm in another world.
JANE SEYMOUR, *Guide to Romantic Living*

The choirs left the main tune and soared two octaves past heaven in a descant to rattle the bones and surge the heart.
HENRY MITCHELL, *on the dedication of the nave of Washington D.C.'s National Cathedral, 1976*

33

What we provide is an atmosphere... of orchestrated pulse which works on people in a subliminal way. Under it's influence I've seen shy debs and severe dowagers kick off their shoes and raise some wholesome hell.

MEYER DAVIS, *on his orchestra*

Music hath charms to soothe the savage beast, but I'd try a revolver first.

JOSH BILLINGS

audiences...

The musical experience needs three human beings at least. It requires a composer, a performer, and a listener; and unless these three take part together there is no musical experience.

BENJAMIN BRITTEN

The audience is the best judge of anything... they cannot be lied to... any touch of falseness, and they retreat from you.

BARBRA STREISAND

Give me the best instrument in Europe, but listeners who understand nothing or do not wish to understand and who do not feel with me in what I am playing, and all my pleasure is spoilt.

WOLFGANG AMADEUS MOZART

34

Can that which has cost the artist days, weeks, months, and even years of reflection be understood in a flash by the dilettante?
ROBERT SCHUMANN

A painter paints his picture on canvas. But musicians paint pictures on silence. We provide the music, and you provide the silence!
LEOPOLD STOKOWSKI, *reprimanding a talkative audience*

A really great reception makes me feel like I have a great big warm heating pad all over me. I truly have a great love for an audience.
JUDY GARLAND

A [Judy Garland] audience doesn't just listen. They have their arms around her when she works.
SPENCER TRACY

What is the voice of song, when the word lacks the ear of taste?
NATHANIEL HAWTHORNE

You have always given me more than I gave to you... You were the wings on which I soared.
LOTTE LEHMANN, *to audience at her farewell concert*

36

Flint must be an extremely wealthy town; I see that each of you bought two or three seats.
VICTOR BORGE, *playing to a half-filled house in Flint, Michigan*

One of the greatest frauds under which we suffer is the maxim "The best things in life are free." Nothing could be further from the truth. In fact the best things in life cost us dearly, and it is for this reason alone that very few strive for them. Take for instance one's knowledge of Beethoven. Only a fool thinks that the appreciation of Beethoven comes free of charge.
JOSEPH PETTICREW

critics...

If one hears bad music it is one's duty to drown it by one's conversation.
OSCAR WILDE

Nothing soothes me more after a long and maddening course of pianoforte recitals than to sit and have my teeth drilled.
GEORGE BERNARD SHAW

I thought of myself as a species of knight-errant, attacking dragons single-handedly and rescuing musical virtue in distress.
VIRGIL THOMSON, *on his role as critic*

Never mind adverse press. It is predominantly the voice of conventionality and exerts, if anything, a negative effect on thinking people. And especially never mind how much applause. It is not so much correlated with the quality of the music as it is a conditioned response elicited by the bravura of a strong personality on stage or the clangor of a loud and vigorous finale.

RICHARD MAXFIELD

Not a single critic understood what had impelled me to compose these works....

DARIUS MILHAUD

Critics can't even make music by rubbing their back legs together.

MEL BROOKS

I have found through my experiences that critics know what you're thinking or trying to portray as much as a baby in Afghanistan would understand when you speak English.

DIZZY GILLESPIE

No statue has ever been put up to a critic.

JEAN SIBELIUS

No two men ever judged alike of the same thing, and it is impossible to find two opinions exactly similar, not only in different men but in the same men at different times.

MICHEL MONTAIGNE

The day I start listening to critics is the day they go out and make an album.

> HELEN REDDY, *on hearing that Rolling Stone voted her Greatest Hits album the worst album of 1976*

about composers...

Keep an eye on that young man, someday he will make a big splash in the world.

> WOLFGANG AMADEUS MOZART, *about Beethoven*

Mozart is just God's way of making the rest of us feel insignificant.

> DAVID W. BARBER, *Bach, Beethoven and the Boys*

You can't possibly hear the last movement of Beethoven's Seventh and go slow.

> OSCAR LEVANT, *explaining his way out of a speeding ticket*

[Mozart's] style combines formal elegance with deep expressiveness. The delight of nuance, the sense of tonal colour and flexibility of style save Mozart's strong vein of lyricism from all Romantic excess and preserve for it the delicacy and supreme elegance of classicism. In its once and for all perfection, Mozart's work arises from the profoundest depths of musical inspiration.

> GEOFFREY HINDLEY

40

No composer in history... [Bach] has been so widely jazzed up, watered down, electrified and otherwise transmogrified, debated and admired as this German provincial.
ALAN RICH, *Newsweek, December 1984*

If I had lost all my religious faith, this thing alone would be sufficient to restore it.
FELIX MENDELSSOHN, *to Robert Schumann after playing one of Bach's choral preludes*

I love Beethoven, especially the poems.
RINGO STARR

For me, the most difficult, the deepest music is in Mozart, Beethoven, Schubert, and Haydn. And therefore, if you're a master in that area, what you have to say about Brahms and Schumann will be very interesting.
EUGENE ISTOMIN

Handel is the greatest composer that ever lived... I would uncover my head and kneel down on his tomb.
LUDWIG VAN BEETHOVEN

The music of Bach is a summing up of the music of some hundred odd years before him. His musical material is themes and motives used by his predecessors... Is this plagiarism? By no means. For an artist it is not only right to have his roots in the art of some former times, it is a necessity.
BÉLA BARTÓK

41

There are two kinds of genius—natural genius and rational genius. Though I admire the latter immensely, I must confess that my whole being responds to the former. Yes, my dear fellow, I make bold to prefer Raphael to Michelangelo, Mozart to Beethoven, and Rossini to Meyerbeer...

GEORGES BIZET

Then he would get carried away, pound the piano, and the strings of the delicate Viennese instruments would pop. No piano was safe with Beethoven... Beethoven broke more pianos than any one in Vienna.

HAROLD SCHÖNBERG

Life can't be all bad when for ten dollars you can buy all the Beethoven sonatas and listen to them for ten years.

WILLIAM F. BUCKLEY, JR.

I occasionally play works by contemporary composers for two reasons. First, to discourage the composer from writing any more and secondly to remind myself how much I appreciate Beethoven.

JASCHA HEIFETZ

His [Beethoven's] music always reminds one of paintings of battles.

BERTOLT BRECHT

Bach opens a vista to the universe. After experiencing him, people feel there is meaning to life after all.

HELMUT WALCHA

42

[Wagner's] music is so complex, and so ingeniously contrived, so interwoven with so many motifs... it is almost physical in its impact.
GEOFFREY HINDLEY

Wagner's music is better than it sounds.
MARK TWAIN

One can't judge Wagner's opera *Lohengrin* after a first hearing, and I certainly don't intend hearing it a second time.
GIOACHINO ROSSINI

Berlioz says nothing in his music, but he says it magnificently.
JAMES GIBBONS HUNEKAR

Brahms is the spirit of Vienna; Strauss is the perfume.
JULES MASSENET

I am equally fond of both artists; but I would dance to Strauss' music with the best dancer, and to Lanner's music with the dearest. The waltzes of Strauss are gayer, those of Lanner more poetical.
KAROLINE BAUER

Brahms' northern heritage deeply pervades his music. It is the sea that surges through all his harmonies, the northern sea with its long, heavy breakers.
EMIL LUDWIG

My musical credo is in the key of E flat major whose key signature has three flats: Bach, Beethoven, Brahms!
HANS VON BÜLOW

He is loved... as a fact of sonic geology, like a throbbing song-filled Rock of Gibraltar.
NED ROREM, *on Aaron Copland*

If a young man at the age of twenty three can write a symphony like that, in five years he will be ready to commit murder.
WALTER DAMROSCH, *on Aaron Copland*

If that's new music, I don't like it! But it is what I meant.
RALPH VAUGHAN WILLIAMS, *after conducting one of his own compositions*

Sousa was no Beethoven. Nonetheless, he was Sousa.
DEEMS TAYLOR

He [Sousa] wrote marches for this [US Marine] band, including *Stars and Stripes Forever,* a neatly assembled flame of controlled fire, guaranteed to make the lame walk.
IAN WHITCOMB, *After the Ball: Popular Song from Rag to Rock*

How far can the composer be held accountable... after all is said and sung?
CHARLES IVES

45

From Gershwin emanated a new American music not written with the ruthlessness of one who strives to demolish established rules, but based on a new native gusto and wit and awareness. His was a modernity that reflected the civilization we live in as excitingly as the headline in today's newspaper.

IRA GERSHWIN, *The Gershwin Years*

... a sort of musical kaleidoscope of America—of our vast melting pot, of our incomparable national pep, our blues, our metropolitan madness.

GEORGE GERSHWIN, *on his own music*

composers on composing...

People compose for many reasons: to become immortal; because the pianoforte happens to be open; because they want to become a millionaire; because of the praise of friends; because they have looked into a pair of beautiful eyes; for no reason whatever.

ROBERT SCHUMANN

I find I cannot write at all unless I write for public approbation and get credit for what I write.

STEPHEN FOSTER

I adore art... when I am alone with my notes, my heart pounds and the tears stream from my eyes, and my emotion and my joys are too much to bear.

GIUSEPPE VERDI

46

As matters now stand with me I am no longer spurred to creative effort by ambition, but by the urge to communicate with my friends and the wish to give them pleasure: whenever I know this urge and wish have been satisfied, I am happy and entirely content.

RICHARD WAGNER, *in a letter to Franz Liszt*

... the product of my genius and my misery, and that which I have written in my greatest distress, is that which the world seems to like best.

FRANZ SCHUBERT

I write [music] as a sow piddles.

WOLFGANG AMADEUS MOZART

It is melancholy to be always a slave: but Providence wills it so. I am an unfortunate creature! Always plagued with much work, very few hours of repose...

FRANZ JOSEPH HAYDN

Artists are fiery, they do not weep!

LUDWIG VAN BEETHOVEN

When I am, as it were, completely myself, entirely alone, and of good cheer—say traveling in a carriage, or walking after a good meal, or during the night when I cannot sleep; it is on such occasions that my ideas flow best and most abundantly. When and how they come, I know not; I cannot force them...

WOLFGANG AMADEUS MOZART

47

I produce music as an apple tree produces apples.
CAMILLE SAINT-SAËNS

Whatever speech I hear, no matter who is speaking nor what he says, my mind is already working to find the musical statement for such speech.
MODEST P. MUSSORGSKY, *in a letter to Rimsky-Korsakov*

Anything that happens in the world affects me; politics for example, literature, people; I reflect about all these things in my own way—and these reflections then seek to find an outlet in music. This is also the reason for which many of my compositions are hard to understand.
ROBERT SCHUMANN

Composing is like driving down a foggy road toward a house. Slowly you see more details of the house, the color and slates and bricks, the shape of the windows. The notes are the bricks and mortar of the house.
BENJAMIN BRITTEN

A man like Verdi, must write like Verdi.
GIUSEPPE VERDI

I find that my creative energy comes and goes, yes. It seems it comes most strongly when I'm falling in love, or when I am moved by political or religious sentiments.
JOAN BAEZ

48

I don't write songs. They come to me and say, "Okay you're the one. I want to put this down."
JOHN DENVER

My songs were there before I came along... I just sort of took them down with a pencil.
BOB DYLAN

I hang my laundry on the line when I write.
JONI MITCHELL

I am the German spirit. Consult the incomparable magic of my works; hold them side by side with everything else; you have no choice but to say—this is German.
RICHARD WAGNER

My sole inspiration is a telephone call from a producer.
COLE PORTER

You compose because you want to somehow summarize in some permanent form your most basic feelings about being alive, to set down... some sort of permanent statement about the way it feels to live now, today.
AARON COPLAND

Every composer knows the anquish and despair occasioned by forgetting ideas which one has no time to write down.
HECTOR BERLIOZ

Young people can learn from my example that something can come out of nothing. What I have become is all the result of dire need.

FRANZ JOSEPH HAYDN, *when asked for advice for youth*

At first I thought I should be a second Beethoven; presently I found that to be another Schubert would be good; then gradually, satisfied with less and less, I resigned to be a Humperdinck.

ENGLEBERT HUMPERDINCK

Clara has written a number of smaller pieces which show a musicianship and a tenderness of invention such as she has never before attained. But children, and a husband who is always living in the realms of imagination, do not go well with composition. She cannot work at it regularly, and I am often disturbed to think how many tender ideas are lost because she cannot work them out.

ROBERT SCHUMANN, *about his wife*

With cries of labor I gave birth to this hymn.

ENHEDUANNA

I have been composing a good deal lately and have called my piano pieces after the names of my favorite haunts, partly because they really came into my mind at these spots...they will form a delightful souvenir, and a kind of second diary.

FANNY MENDELSSOHN HENSEL, *in a letter to sister Rebecca*

51

Now I am going to Vienna, and in January to Switzerland, continuing my amphibian life, half virtuoso, half composer. Just now the virtuoso is winning praise, which does not say much for the composer...

JOHANNES BRAHMS, *in a letter to Joseph Joachim*

My sole ambition as a composer is to hurl my javelin into the infinite space of the future.

FRANZ LISZT

The real composer thinks about his work the whole time; he is not always conscious of this, but he is aware of it later when he suddenly knows what he will do... I love whatever I am now doing, and with each new work I feel that I have at last found the way, have just begun to compose.

IGOR SRAVINSKY

Don't bother to look, I've composed all this already.

GUSTAV MAHLER, *to Bruno Walter who had stopped to admire mountain scenery in rural Austria*

... such incidents brought me to the verge of despair, but little more and I would have put an end to my life— only art it was that withheld me, — ah, it seemed impossible to leave the world until I had produced all that I had felt called upon to produce.

LUDWIG VAN BEETHOVEN, *Heiligenstadt Testament*

52

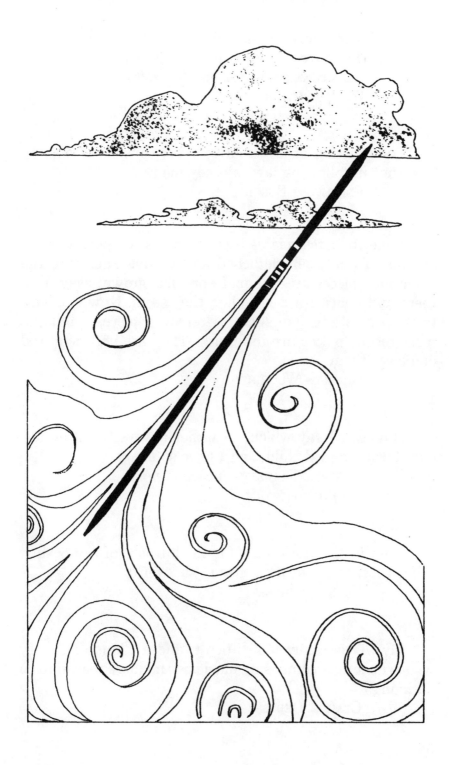

Strict adherence to the rules of composition is, paradoxically, the source of the composer's freedom.

ALLAN JANIK and STEPHEN TOULMIN,
Wittgenstein's Vienna

The function of the creative artist consists of making laws, not in following laws already made.

FERRUCCIO BUSONI

I like the latest pieces best. All one's compositions are chunks of one's self detached and frozen. Therefore the older such pieces are, the more one has grown away from them and hence the more alien they seem. Now it is perfectly possible to like such far-removed pieces... but the most recent pieces are different. They are children, and one loves them.

CHARLES WUORINEN

How can I say which? A father always has a preference for a crippled child, and I have so many.

GAETANO DONIZETTI, *asked to name his favourite opera*

I am in the world only for the purpose of composing. What I feel in my heart, I give to the world.

FRANZ SCHUBERT

My life is really too difficult, and a Claude Debussy who is no longer composing music has no more reason to go on living.

CLAUDE DEBUSSY

54

A great work is made out of a combination of obedience and liberty.

NADIA BOULANGER

From the heart, may it again go to the heart.

LUDWIG VAN BEETHOVEN, *words inscribed on the manuscript of Missa Solemnis*

I know that the twelve notes in each octave and the varieties of rhythm offer me opportunities that all of human genius will never exhaust.

IGOR STRAVINSKY

There are still so many beautiful things to be said in C major.

SERGEI PROKOFIEV

conductors...

I never use a score when conducting my orchestra... Does a lion tamer enter a cage with a book on how to tame a lion?

DIMITRI MITROPOLOUS

To the sound itself... the conductor adds the italics and punctuation of gesture, of strained arms, of startling tautness of the shoulders, of brisk nod, of hands flung apart in some wild appeal to the universe.

CHRISTOPHER ANDREAE

55

I use my hands like a sculptor, to mold and shape the sound I want to clarify.

LEONARD SLATKIN

God tells me how the music should sound, but you stand in the way.

ARTURO TOSCANINI, *to a trumpet player*

I'm one of the boys, no better than the last second violinist... I'm just the lucky one to be standing in the center, telling them how to play.

EUGENE ORMANDY

Already too loud!

BRUNO WALTER, *at his first rehearsal with an American orchestra, on seeing the players reaching for their instruments*

A work of art does not answer questions, it provokes them; and its essential meaning is in the tension between the contradictory answers.

LEONARD BERNSTEIN

Essentially, the [New York] Philharmonic is just like any other orchestra—they all have the spirit of kids, and if you scratch away a little of the fatigue and cynicism, out comes a 17 year old music student again, full of wonder, exuberance and a tremendous love of music.

ZUBIN MEHTA

56

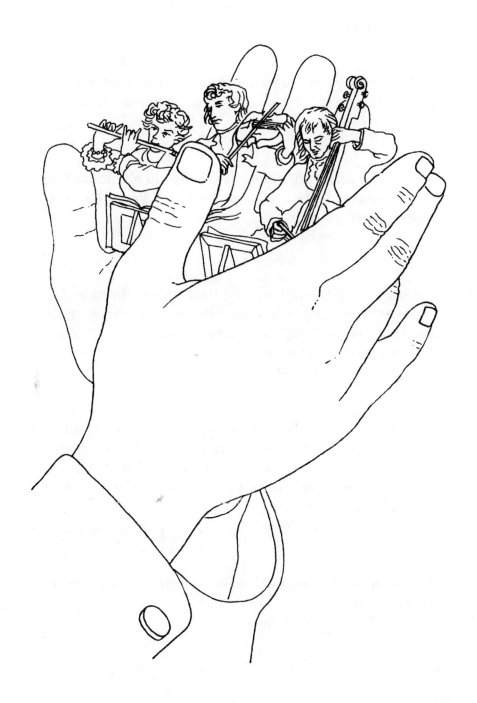

Gentlemen, I would ask those of you who are married to play this phrase as if you were engaged.
RICHARD STRAUSS

There's only one woman I know of who could never be a symphony conductor, and that's the Venus de Milo.
MARGARET HILLIS

The conductor must make it possible to eliminate himself in the music. If the orchestra feels him doing that, then everything will go well.
GIUSEPPE SINOPOLI

It's a strange thing! When I hear music—even while I am conductig—I hear quite positive answers to my questions, and feel perfectly clear and confident. Or rather, I feel quite clearly that there are no questions...
GUSTAV MAHLER

Never try to tell a man how to play his instrument: he knows far more about it than you do, and will immediately resent your effort. Instead, explain exactly what it is you want, and leave it to him to produce the desired tone, effect, or whatever it is.
SIR ADRIAN BOULT

You know why conductors live so long? because we perspire so much.
SIR JOHN BARBIROLLI

58

All the world's a performance. A monkey performs, lovers perform, Picasso's drawings are a marvel of performance, and the President of the United States performs his office. The work is growing old under my pen. Give me young words...

LUKAS FOSS

Mendelssohn had the gift without which no artist, no matter how talented, can succeed: the ability to come over the footlights, to impress one's personality on the hearer.

JOHN EDMUND COX

When a performer lacks personality we call the performance dull; when he has too much personality we complain that he obscures the piece from view.

AARON COPLAND

Genius is an overused word. The world has known only about a half a dozen geniuses. I have achieved only a medium approach to my ideal in music. I got only fairly near.

FRITZ KREISLER

Man's peculiar privilege is walking erect, on two feet and thereby being forced to stretch his hands upward to heaven. This conquering of gravity, space and height, as well as of horizon, is essential in violin playing.

SIR YEHUDI MENUHIN

59

A violin should be played with love, or not at all.
JOSEPH WECHSBERG

pianists...

Liszt came on stage, shook his mane, lifted his hands high and came crashing down on the keys. Strings snapped, great volumes of tone filled the air, and a new world of pianistic color and excitement was discovered as the king of virtuosos swept up and down the keyboard... His recitals sent the ladies into a bacchanalian frenzy.
HAROLD SCHÖNBERG, *The Great Pianists*

I cannot tell you how much I love to play for people. Would you believe it—sometimes when I sit down to practice and there is no one else in the room, I have to stifle an impulse to ring for the elevator man and offer him money to come in and hear me.
ARTHUR RUBINSTEIN

When she [Wanda Landowska] held on to a fermata, worlds tottered and the sun stopped until she went on to the next phrase.
HAROLD SCHÖNBERG

My mission will be to have introduced poetry into piano music with some brilliance. You see, my piano is for me, what his ship is to a sailor; more indeed: it is my very self, my mother tongue, my life.
FRANZ LISZT

60

Keyboardists whose chief asset is mere technique... more often than not astound us with their prowess without ever touching our sensibilities. They overwhelm our hearing without satisfying it and stun the mind without moving it.

C. P. E. BACH

I am not fitted to give concerts. The audience intimidates me, I feel choked by its breath, paralyzed by its curious glances, struck dumb by all those strange faces.

FREDERIC CHOPIN

I beg you, my dear friend, when you do me the honor of playing my compositions, to play them as they are written or else not at all.

FREDERIC CHOPIN, *to Liszt*

Play it yourself then! ...Ah yes, my friend, you were right; works like yours ought not to be meddled with; other people's alterations only spoil them. You are a true poet.

FRANZ LISZT, *to Chopin*

My whole trick is to keep the tune well out in front. If I play Tchaikovsky, I play his melodies and skip his spiritual struggle.

LIBERACE

When she started to play, Steinway himself came down personally and rubbed his name off the piano.

BOB HOPE, *on comedienne Phyllis Diller*

62

I really don't know whether any place contains more pianists than Paris, or whether you can find more asses and virtuosos anywhere.
FREDERIC CHOPIN

I have no style, because I change each time... each day I play differently. Today I play differently than yesterday.
VLADIMIR HOROWITZ

singers...

Every time she [Edith Piaf] sings you have the feeling she's wrenching her soul from her body for the last time.
JEAN COCTEAU

For me, singing is a way of escaping. It's another world. I'm no longer on earth.
EDITH PIAF

I was bathed in music from the beginning, and I cannot conceive of life without it.
KIRSTEN FLAGSTAD

There is something about the creative process... which is that you can't talk about it. You try to think of anecdotes about it, and you try to explain, but you're never really saying what happened... it's a sort of happy accident.
BETTY COMDEN

63

The strange thing about a singer's destiny is that you have to renounce everything for its sake, and then it's all over in a flash. The imprint we leave is like the snow you see falling this afternoon. Tomorrow it will be gone, and there will be nothing. Yes, a few people will remember, but only for a very short time.
LISA DELLA CASA

Only when I was singing did I feel loved.
MARIA CALLAS

A superb tenor voice, like a trumpet muffled in silk.
SIR ALEC GUINNESS, *on Sir John Gielgud*

Yes, of course. Some are violins, some are fountain pens and some are stethoscopes. And others are just washboards.
MARILYN VOS SAVANT, *when asked if the voice is an instrument*

The eternal task of song can never be finished in a single lifetime. That is the beauty and fascination of the art. Once you begin to phrase finely, you will feel more joy in the beautiful finish of a beautiful phrase than that caused by the loudest applause of an immense audience. The latter excites for a moment; the former endures forever.
DAME NELLIE MELBA

The buck stops here. I don't share blame, I don't share credit, and I don't share desserts.
BEVERLY SILLS

Rich, supple and shining, it was in its prime capable of effortlessly soaring from a smoky mezzo to the pure soprano gold of a perfectly spun high C.

MICHAEL WALSH, *on the voice of Leontyne Price*

I am an inexact artist. When I go out on the stage, I live the music, and this is what counts for me. Technique has never concerned me, for I am a creature of the instinct. So what if I hit a wrong note?

LOTTE LEHMANN

My essential purpose in singing is to help the listener understand reality.

PETE SEEGER

The only reality in music is the state of mind which it induces in the listener.

STENDHAL

songs...

Swans sing before they die—'twere no bad thing
Did certain persons die before they sing.

SAMUEL TAYLOR COLERIDGE

It is the best of all trades, to make songs, and the second best to sing them.

HILAIRE BELLOC

66

Laugh and be merry, remember, better the world with a song.

JOHN MASEFIELD

No song, no supper.

LATIN PROVERB

Life is a shipwreck but we must not forget to sing in the lifeboats.

VOLTAIRE

Ballad singing has been going on ever since people sang at all. It comes up like an underground stream and then goes back again. But it always exists.

BURL IVES

Come sing now, sing; for I know ye sing well,
I see ye have a singing face.

FRANCIS BEAUMONT and JOHN FLETCHER

He who sings scares away his woes.

MIGUEL DE CERVANTES

Any song that moves you to joy or tears has greatness.

MARGUERITE PIAZZA

instruments...

I want to make the piano not a percussive instrument, but a singing instrument. The piano has to sing as much as it can.
VLADIMIR HOROWITZ

The piano's world encompasses glass-nerved virtuosi and stomping barrel-housers in fedoras: it is a world of pasture and storm, of perfumed smoke, of liquid mathematics.... No other acoustic instrument can match its expressive range, and no electric instrument can match its mystery.
KENNETH MILLER

It happens very rarely, but when it happens it's worth waiting for, that the instrument becomes part of your body.
JACK BRYMER

[It is my] wooden wife.
MSTISLAV ROSTROPOVICH, *on his Stradivarius*

The oboe sounds like a clarinet with a cold, but it is the instrument the whole orchestra tunes up to.
VICTOR BORGE

I can see fiddling around with a banjo, but how do you banjo around with a fiddle?
DUNCAN PURNEY

68

The thing that influenced me most was the way Tommy played his trombone... It was my idea to make my voice work in the same way as a trombone or violin, not sounding like them, but 'playing' the voice like those instrumentalists.

FRANK SINATRA

The cello is like a beautiful woman who has not grown older, but younger with time, more slender, more supple, more graceful.

PABLO CASALS

Never look at the trombones, it only encourages them.

RICHARD STRAUSS

opera...

At the theatre, we see and hear what has been said, thought and done by various people elsewhere; at the opera we see and hear what was never said, thought or done anywhere but at the opera.

WILLIAM HAZLITT, *The Opera*

Any subject is good for opera if the composer feels it so intently he must sing it out.

GIAN CARLO MENOTTI

In opera, there is always too much singing.

CLAUDE DEBUSSY

69

There is no question but our grandchildren will be very curious to know the reason why their forefathers used to sit together like an audience of foreigners in their own country, and to hear whole plays acted before them in a tongue which they did not understand.

JOSEPH ADDISON, *The Spectator*

An exotic and irrational entertainment.

SAMUEL JOHNSON'S, *definition of opera*

You see actresses virtually in convulsions as they rend from their lungs the most violent ululations; both fists clenched against the breast, the head thrown back, cheeks aflame, veins bursting, and diaphragm heaving. ...what is still more astonishing is that the howls and cries are almost the only thing applauded by the audience.

JEAN JACQUES ROUSSEAU

Opera is where a guy gets stabbed in the back, and instead of dying, he sings.

ROBERT BENCHLEY

The crowning glory of opera is the big ensemble.

W.H. AUDEN

The voice soared majestically, hugely, in the role, flooding the house with opulent, gleaming tones.

THOR ECKERT JR., *on Eva Marton at the Met*

70

Music in the theatre is a powerful, an almost immorally potent weapon.

MARC BLITZSTEIN

I have heard Toscanini conduct Falstaff and Flagstad sing Isolde—the only time that I cried at the opera.

A.J.P. TAYLOR

Bed is the poor man's opera.

ITALIAN PROVERB

Recordings had won him [Enrico Caruso] the affections of millions, who sat by their phonographs and thrilled to the impassioned arias. His countryman wept in exile over nostalgic folk songs winewarm with sunlight... To New York's little Italy he was far more than a voice; he had become a symbol of hope and laughter in adversity. They identified fiercely, patriotically, with the chubby little man who had escaped from a Neapolitan slum to win story book success on alien soil but still spoke broken English and remained as Italian as macaroni.

STANLEY JACKSON, *Caruso*

If a thing isn't worth saying, you sing it.

PIERRE BEAUMARCHAIS, *The Barber of Seville*

Give my love to Kirsten Flagstad and again express to her my great admiration. I suppose the period of my administration will be known in years to come as the time that Flagstad sang in New York.

FIORELLO LA GUARDIA, *in a letter to Ziegler*

72

People are generally amazed that I would take an interest in any form that would require me to stop talking for three hours.

HENRY KISSINGER, *on his fondness for opera*

I'd hate this to get out but I really like opera.

FORD FRICK

Oh how wonderful, really wonderful opera would be if there were no singers!

GIOACHINO ROSSINI

A masterpiece, Evita is a quite marvelous modern opera... Lloyd Webber's score, so full of glorious melodies... is an unparalleled fusion of twentieth century musical experience.

JONATHAN MANTLE, *quoting the London Times in Fanfare*

jazz...

Jazz may be thought of as a current that bubbled forth from a spring in the slums of New Orleans to become the mainstream of the twentieth century.

HENRY PLEASANTS

I want to communicate with people, but I won't put on funny hats to do it.

STAN GETZ

I don't like jazz. When I hear jazz, its as if I had gas on the stomach. I used to think it was static when I heard it on the radio.
NIKITA KHRUSHCHEV

Classical music is being ousted by jazz...
MAXIM GORKY, *describing what he felt to be the decay of Western Culture*

A jazz musician is a juggler who uses harmonies instead of oranges.
BENNY GREEN

If you're going to play good jazz you've got to have a plan of what's going to happen. There has to be intent. It's like an act of murder: you play with an intent to commit something.
DUKE ELLINGTON

Music is your own experience, your thoughts, your wisdom. If you don't live it, it won't come out of your horn.
CHARLIE PARKER

Soul is when you can take a song and make it part of you—a part that's so true, so real, people think it must have happened to you. I'm not satisfied unless I can make them feel what I feel. It's like electricity; it's a force that can light up a room. Soul is power.
RAY CHARLES

74

I'll play it first and tell you what it is later.
MILES DAVIS

I merely took the energy it takes to pout and wrote some blues.
DUKE ELLINGTON, *when asked how he felt about his band being kept out of top spots because of racial prejudices*

I had rather sound like the ashcans of the early morning, like the cab drivers cursing at one another, like the long shoreman yelling, like the cowhands whooping and like the lone wolf barking.
WOODY GUTHRIE

Jazz has contributed an enduring value to America in the sense that it has expressed ourselves.
GEORGE GERSHWIN

What we play is life.
LOUIS ARMSTRONG

pop...

We are surrounded by such a melange of melodies and rhythms, persistently weaving their spells into the fabric of our lives, that it is now possible to feel, for all it's glories, music can and does become something of an intrusion.
RICHARD LEWIS

76

Movie music is noise. It's even more painful than my sciatica.
SIR THOMAS BEECHAM

If few composers today speak of reaching out to the masses with their music... it is because we are increasingly deluged by the products of a people's cultured democracy. The masses have their music, and if anyone doubts it or doubts how they revel in it, he need merely, as I have, be driven by car across or up and down this country and listen to the radio.
MILTON BABBITT

I recommend you to think when at work, not only of the musical but also of the unmusical public. You know that for ten true connoisseurs there are a hundred ignoramuses! Do not neglect the so-called popular, which tickles long ears.
LEOPOLD MOZART, *to his son, Wolfgang when he was working on Idomeneo*

I will yield to popular demands only insofar as they do not betray my own convictions.
CLARA SCHUMANN

Concert audiences need more than familiarity with and exposure to new music. They need self-confidence when they listen. Ultimately, it is up to them whether they like or dislike what they hear.
EARLE BROWNE

77

Listen, kid, take my advice, never hate a song that has sold a half-million copies!

IRVING BERLIN, *to Cole Porter*

I think popular music in this country is one of the few things in the twentieth century that have made giant strides in reverse.

BING CROSBY

Keep it simple, keep it sexy, keep it sad.

MITCH MILLER, *on popular music*

Pop is the perfect religious vehicle. It's as if God has come down to earth and seen all the ugliness that was being created and chosen pop to be the great force for love and beauty.

DONOVAN LEITCH

rock...

People think the Beatles know what's going on. We don't. We're just doing it.

JOHN LENNON

The plaintive and derisive songs of an oppressed people have become the backround for a whole society's pleasures and distractions.

GEOFFREY GOVER, *on the influence of Afro-American rhythms on the world's conception of how music ought to sound*

78

We always knew something would happen sooner or later. We always had this blind Bethlehem star ahead of us. Fame is what everyone wants, in some form or another.
PAUL MCCARTNEY

Ours is the folk music of the technological age.
JIMMY PAGE

We're the poets of Now. You read Yeats or what's his name and you can't make out a word.
GRAHAM NASH

My moment of glory is being on the stage and singing and feeling all the love the audience sends to me... It's beyond any mortal high.
ELVIS PRESLEY, *in If I Can Dream*

Theirs [the Beatles] is a happy, cocky, belligerently resourceless brand of harmonic primitivism... In the Liverpudlian repertoire, the indulgent amateurishness of the musical material, though closely rivaled by the indifference of the performing style, is actually surpassed only by the ineptitude of the studio production method. [*"Strawberry Fields"* suggests a chance encounter at a mountain wedding between Claudio Monteverdi and a jug band.]
GLENN GOULD

I want to tell the world how the guy in the filling station feels.
JOHN LOUDERMILK

79

It's pretty clear now that what looked like it might have been some kind of counterculture is, in reality, just the plain old chaos of undifferentiated weirdness.
JERRY GARCIA

I'm not kidding myself. My voice alone is just an ordinary voice. What people come to see is how I use it. If I stand still while I'm singing, I'm dead, man, I might as well go back to driving a truck.
ELVIS PRESLEY

They seemed on the surface to project the hang loose pose of California's easy living surfdom. But in reality they were serious, well trained musicians, whose surfing image was by no means accurate. Only Dennis surfed regularly.
GEORGE T. SIMON, *on The Beach Boys*

We are a subliminal plugged-in group with coded messages of love.
BRIAN WILSON

Bonded by genetic glue, the voices of the Gibb Brothers kiss notes like three suitors seeking the same lips.
GREG MITCHELL, *describing The Bee Gees superb vocal blend*

I love being a star more than life itself.
JANIS JOPLIN

80

You can get caught up in the visceral charge of its engines, sing along with its chunky tunes and dream its romantic dreams and still feel the cold wind of history blowing through its pages.

STEPHEN HOLDEN, *on Bruce Springsteen and The E Street Band live*

When you're singing and playing rock'n'roll you're on the leading edge of yourself.

NIEL YOUNG

A ponderous orchestral absurdity.

FRANK ZAPPA, *on his rock symphony debuted by the Los Angeles Philharmonic conducted by Zubin Mehta*

We take the kids away from their parents and their environment, to where the only reality is the beat and the rhythm.

MARK FARNER

It has no beginning and no end, for it is the very pulse of life itself.

LARRY WILLIAMS, *on rock'n'roll*

I believe everything is going on in rock. I'm sure it's got a lot to add to the serious music world.

ANDREW LLOYD-WEBBER

82

The Beatles, yes, but the rest is faddism.
DAVID SOYER

advice to musicians...

The indefatigable pursuit of an unattainable perfection, even though it consists in nothing more than the pounding of an old piano, is what alone gives a meaning to our life on this unavailing star.
LOGAN PEARSALL SMITH

Talents are best nurtured in solitude; character is best formed in the stormy billows of the world.
JOHANN WOLFGANG GOETHE

Genius is talent in which character makes itself heard.
LUDWIG WITTGENSTEIN

The advice I am giving always to all my students is above all to study the music profoundly. Because the music is like the ocean, and the instruments are little or bigger islands, very beautiful for the flowers and trees, or the contrary.
ANDRÉS SEGOVIA

Good art is nothing more than infinite patience.
WILLIAM WALLACE KIMBALL

83

All the performances of human art, at which we look with praise and wonder, are instances of the resistless force of perseverence.

BEN JONSON

Of all the work that produces results, nine tenths must be drudgery. There is no work, from the highest to the lowest, which can be done well by any man who is unwilling to make that sacrifice. Part of the very nobility of the devotion of the true workman to his work consists in the fact that a man is not daunted by finding that drudgery must be done.... And there is nothing which so truly repays itself as this very perseverence against weariness.

EDWARD HENRY BICKERSTETH

Knowledge is not skill. Knowledge plus 10,000 times is skill.

SHINICHI SUZUKI

Can you see how the notes behave like waves? Up and down they go! Look, you can also see the mountains. You have to amuse yourself sometimes after being serious for so long.

FRANZ JOSEPH HAYDN

I devote the greater part of my time, four or five hours daily, exclusively to the cultivation of technique.... I crucify, like a good Christ, the flesh of my fingers, in order to make them obedient, submissive machines to the mind, as a pianist must.

HANS VON BÜLOW

84

The artist's first rule is that skill is a tool;
But your art's put to shame if skill is your aim.
FRIEDRICH WIECK

I never practice, I always play.
WANDA LANDOWSKA

Making music, in fact, is the very best way of learning about music.
RICHARD BAKER

Take a child's hands, guide them over the piano keys to pick out a well-known tune, and from that moment he will have a heightened interest in music.
JASCHA HEIFETZ

The study of fingering is a treacherous path along which many have erred... More is lost through poor fingering than can be replaced by all conceivable artistry and good taste.
C. P. E. BACH

You must practice scales and other finger exercises industriously. There are people, however, who think they may achieve great ends by doing this; up to an advanced age, for many hours daily, they practice mechanical exercises. That is as reasonable as trying to recite the alphabet faster and faster every day. Find a better use for your time.
ROBERT SCHUMANN

Keine passagen! Why hurry over beautiful things? Why not linger and enjoy them?

CLARA SCHUMANN, *when students would rattle through rapid configurations with "mere empty virtuosity"*

Dragging and hurrying are equally great faults.

ROBERT SCHUMANN

There is nothing to it. You only have to hit the right note at the right time, and the instrument plays itself.

JOHANN SEBASTIAN BACH

Every difficulty slurred over will be a ghost to disturb your repose later on.

FREDERIC CHOPIN

A calm mind and clear vision are attained in a quiet body, and only the quiet and focusing mind can perceive the ticking of a clock or produce an exquisite tone on a musical instrument.

WILLIAM and CONSTANCE STARR

He [Louis Armstrong] also taught me by his example that the key to music, the key to life, is concentration.

BOBBY HACKETT

Never compete, create.

EARL NIGHTINGALE

86

Regard your voice as capital in the bank. When you go to sing, do not draw on your bank account. Sing on your interest and your voice will last.

LAURITZ MELCHIOR

I don't know the key to success, but the key to failure is trying to please everybody.

BILL COSBY

Don't do unto others as you would have them do unto you, their tastes may be different.

GEORGE BERNARD SHAW

I don't want to appeal to everybody. [After all] everybody doesn't appeal to me.

EYDIE GORME

Creativity is harnessing universality and making it flow through your eyes... The greatest happiness in life is to be truly and consistently creative.

PETER KOESTENBAUM

There are no casual notes in music. If this is not the way you choose to speak; if you cannot say more this way than you can with words, do not be a musician.

ISAAC STERN, *in the film*
From Mao to Mozart

Hug a musician, they never get to dance.

MARILYN CAMPBELL

88

music, truth, beauty...

...There lies the truth.
*The dying Beethoven, pointing to
his collection of Handel's works*

There is no truer truth obtainable by man than comes of music.
ROBERT BROWNING

Music tells no truth.
P.J. BAILEY

But truth is so great a thing that we ought not to despise any medium that will conduct us to it.
MICHEL MONTAIGNE

[The piano is] able to communicate the subtlest universal truths by means of wood, metal and vibrating air.
KENNETH MILLER

Listen, I will now tell you the truth and there is no other.
ISAAC STERN, *on what every
conductor says to his artists*

The 'beautiful' in music is a by-product of the composer's integrity, a function of his search for the truth.
ARNOLD SCHÖNBERG

89

The human soul needs actual beauty even more than bread. The middle classes jeer at the colliers for buying pianos—but what is the piano, often as not, but a blind reaching out for beauty?

D. H. LAWRENCE

Sure there is music even in the beauty, and the silent note which Cupid strikes, sweeter far than the sound of an instrument. For there is music wherever there is a harmony, order, or proportion: and thus we may maintain the music of the spheres.

SIR THOMAS BROWNE

music, emotions, spirit...

Our modernized minds need to be musicalized. We have deified the intellect... and developed only half of man's possibilities. There is no other human activity that asks for such a harmonius cooperation of 'intellect' and 'soul' as artistic creation, especially music.

ERNST LEVY

Music was a thing of the soul—a rose lipped shell that murmured of the eternal sea—a strange bird singing the songs of another shore.

J. G. HOLLAND

Music... the favorite passion of my soul.

THOMAS JEFFERSON

90

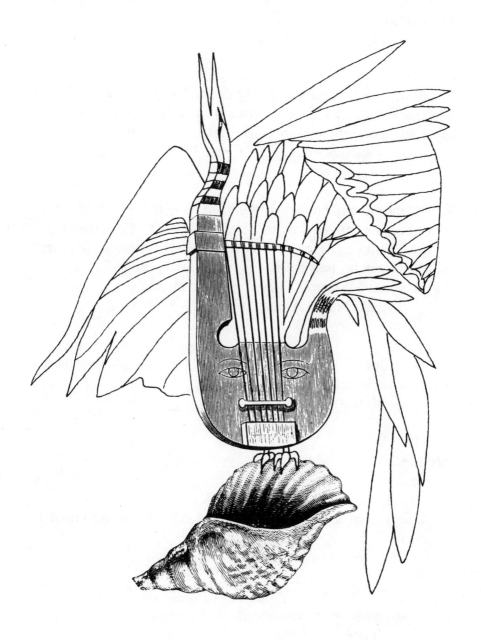

Music appeals to the heart, whereas writing is addressed to the intellect; it communicates ideas directly, like perfume.

HONORÉ DE BALZAC

Many musicians are easily excited into joy, and easily depressed into gloom. This comes from their sensitive natures without which they could not be musicians.

PERCY SCHOLES, *The Great Musicians*

In music the passions, whether violent or not, should never be so expressed as to reach the point of causing disgust; and music, even in situations of the greatest horror, should never be painful to the ear, but should flatter and charm it, and thereby always remain music.

WOLFGANG AMADEUS MOZART

It is music's lofty mission to shed light on the depths of the human heart.

ROBERT SCHUMANN

silence...

The music in my heart I bore, long after it was heard no more.

WILLIAM WORDSWORTH

The pause is as important as the note.

TRUMAN FISHER

92

Music, when soft voices die
Vibrates in the memory—
  PERCY BYSSHE SHELLEY

He who hears music, feels his solitude peopled at once.
  ROBERT BROWNING

No voice, but oh! the silence sank
Like music on my heart.
  SAMUEL TAYLOR COLERIDGE

Everybody should have his personal sounds to listen for—sounds that will make him exhilarated and alive or quiet and calm... One of the greatest sounds of them all—and to me it is a sound—is utter, complete silence.
  ANDRE KOSTELANETZ

Music and silence... combine strongly because music is done with silence, and silence is full of music.
  MARCEL MARCEAU

Silence is the fabric upon which the notes are woven.
  LAWRENCE DUNCAN

After silence, that which comes nearest to expressing the inexpressible is music.
  ALDOUS HUXLEY

93

immortality...

I remember loving sound before I ever took a music lesson. And so we make our lives by what we love.
JOHN CAGE

Recall the lives of Beethoven and Shakespeare, Mozart and Tolstoy, Tchaikovsky and Dickens, those titans of the human mind and spirit, were they not great precisely because they followed the dictates of their consciences and devoted their talents to the service of man? Is it not this that has made them immortal?
SERGEI PROKOFIEV

I will sing to the Lord all my life, make music to my God while I live.
PSALM 103

Songs have an immunity from death.
OVID

Never did Mozart write for eternity, and it is for precisely this reason that much of what he wrote is for eternity.
ALBERT EINSTEIN

It is at once by poetry and through poetry, by music and through music, that the soul divines what splendors shine behind the tomb...
EDGAR ALLAN POE

94

Music is enough for a lifetime—but a lifetime is not enough for music.
SERGEY RAKHMANINOV

Let me have music dying, and I seek no more delight.
JOHN KEATS

Music has here entombed a rich treasure—
But still fairer hopes
FRANZ SCHUBERT, *epitaph*

It won't be long before we'll be writing together again. I just hope they have a decent piano up there.
FREDERICK LOEWE, *in a letter read at Alan Jay Lerner's memorial service*

I enjoy life. I think I'll enjoy death even more. Life is too confusing.
CAT STEVENS

I have dared and done, for my resting place is found, The C major of this life: so now I will try to sleep.
ROBERT BROWNING

Where is music going? Nowhere now. Eventually, though, it will follow, as it has in the past, wherever a great master leads it.
NED ROREM

95

Play Mozart in memory of me.
> FREDERIC CHOPIN, *dying words*

Music that gentlier on the spirit lies,
Than tired eyelids upon tired eyes.
> ALFRED LORD TENNYSON

Let me die to the sounds of delicious music.
> HONORÉ MIRABEAU, *last words*

The future of music may not lie entirely in music itself, but rather in the way it encourages and extends, rather than limits, the aspirations and ideals of the people, in the way it makes itself a part with the finer things that humanity does and dreams of.
> CHARLES IVES

Music was born free, and to win freedom is its destiny.
> FERRUCCHIO BUSONI

I always wish that the last movement [of the *Regenlieder Sonata*] might accompany me in my journey from here to the next world.
> CLARA SCHUMANN

But why so many words about music? The best discourse on music is silence... Away with your musical journals!
> ROBERT SCHUMANN

Name Index

Acknowledgements

We are grateful to the following for permission to reproduce copyright material:

Frederick Yohe for the excerpt from his poem *"Someone Is About To Happen To You"* © Little Brown and Company (1973). Richard Bach for the excerpt of *"The Bridge Across Forever"* © William Morrow & Company & Alternative Futures (1984). Richard Brautigan for the excerpt from his poem *"Gee Your So Beautiful That It's Starting To Rain"* taken from *"The Pill Verses The Springfield Mine Disaster"* © Doubleday/Delacorte press & The Helen Brann Agency Inc. (1968). Wallace Stevens for the excerpt from his poem *"Peter Quince at the Clavier"* © Alfred A. Knopf and Faber & Faber reprinted from *"The Collected Works of Wallace Stevens"* © (1923, revised 1951).

Every reasonable effort has been made to contact and acknowledge copyright holders of material used in this book. Both the author and the publisher welcome any information regarding errors or omissions so that necessary corrections can be made in subsequent printing.

THE MUSIC LOVER'S QUOTATION BOOK
A Lyrical Companion

Published in Canada by:
SOUND AND VISION
359 Riverdale Avenue
Toronto, Canada
M4J 1A4

This book originally published in a
hard cover edition, October 1990.
First paperback printing January 1992

This edition printed December 1996
14 12 10 8 6 - printings - 7 9 11 13 15

Canadian Cataloguing in Publication Data

Main entry under title:
The Music lover's quotation book
ISBN 0-920151-14-0
1. Music - Quotations, maxims, etc Kimball, Kathleen,
   1954 - . II. Petersen, Robin. Johnson, Kathleen
   PN6084.M8M88 1990   780   C90-094982-1

Printed and bound in Canada

Other Music books from Sound And Vision:

A Musician's Dictionary
by David W. Barber & Dave Donald
isbn 0-920151-03-5

Bach, Beethoven and the Boys
Music History as It Ought to Be Taught
isbn 0-920151-10-8

When the Fat Lady Sings
Opera History as It Ought to Be Taught
by David W. Barber & Dave Donald
isbn 0-920151-11-6

If it Ain't Baroque
More Music History as It Ought to Be Taught
by David W. Barber & Dave Donald
isbn 0-920151-15-9

Getting a Handel on Messiah
by David W. Barber & Dave Donald
isbn 0-920151-17-5

Tenors, Tantrums and Trills
An Opera Dictionary from Aida to Zzzz
by David W. Barber & Dave Donald
isbn 0-920151-19-1

Love Lives of the Great Composers
from Gesualdo to Wagner
by Basil Howitt
isbn 0-920151-18-3

How to Stay Awake
During Anybody's Second Movement
by David E. Walden
isbn 0-92015120-5

I Wanna Be Sedated
Pop Music in the Seventies
by Phil Dellio & Scott Woods
isbn 0-920151-16-7

If you have any comments on this book or any other book
we publish, please write to us at Sound And Vision,
359 Riverdale Avenue, Toronto M4J 1A4, Canada
or Email us at musicbooks@soundandvision.com.